07 10 1 *~~~~

Sue

Priceless Proverbs

Kristi Porter

KRISTI PORTER

Copyright © 2014 Happi Kamper Press

ISBN: 0692291601
ISBN-13: 978-0692291603

CONTENTS

Dedication

This book is dedicated to every parent, grandparent, and caregiver that entrusted me with the care and education of their child over the years.

We've all earned a good laugh.

And to the Happi Kamper Kids, the preschoolers at Community United Methodist Preschool, and the Power Play Kids, who all had a part in providing me with material for this book.

Keep smiling and providing those laughs!

The Story Behind This Book

Priceless Proverbs is the result of hundreds of interviews with young children ages three to twelve, who were presented with the first half of a famous saying or proverb and then asked to finish it themselves.

It began as part of a larger class project by teacher Kristi Porter and the children of Happi Kamper Child Care, located in North Muskegon, Michigan. Each child was to create an individual gift book for his or her parents, and Priceless Proverbs was simply to be one chapter in each child's book.

Now, the individual answers of the Happi Kamper Kids, as well as those of the children at Community United Methodist Preschool, and Power Play Childcare in N. Muskegon have been combined. Their diverse, candid, and often priceless answers may surprise you, or even make you laugh out loud, as you get a quick glimpse into the amazing and intricate minds of some of the most delightful and fascinating children around. Enjoy!

OLD ENGLISH

AND OTHER

FAMOUS

PROVERBS

It's better to be safe than...
... to talk to my mom when she's mad! Kelcie, age 3.

~~~~~~

Children should be seen and not...
... play Hulk in the house. Mason, age 4.

~~~~~~

It's always darkest before...
... the monsters come. Cole, age 4.

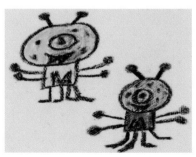

~~~~~~

You can lead a horse to water but...
... then he will have to pee. Kacey, age 4.

~~~~~~

No News is...
... when you catch the TV on fire. Lorna, age 4.

~~~~~~

A bird in the hand is worth...
... getting bird poop on you. Nick, age 4.

~~~~~~

Two's company, three's...
... more company, and 18 is a party! William, age 5.

~~~~~~~~~~~~~~~~~~~~~~~~~~~~~~~~~~~~~

What's good for the goose, is...
... goose food.   Ava, age 4.

~~~~~~~~~~~~~~~~~~~~~~~~~~~~~~~~~~~~~

It's never too late to...
... go somewhere fun. Devin, age 8.

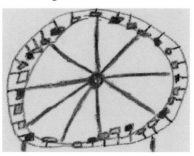

~~~~~~~~~~~~~~~~~~~~~~~~~~~~~~~~~~~~~

Give a man enough rope and...
… he will get it in a big knot. Adam, age 4.

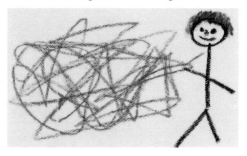

~~~~~~

The early bird gets...
…wet feet, 'cause the grass is still wet. Dylan, age 5.

~~~~~~~~~~~~~~~~~~~~~~~~~~~~~~~~~~~~~~~

A miss is as good as a...
… married.   Ashley, age 4.

~~~~~~

If you can't beat them…
… put your running shoes on! Jaley, age 4.

~~~~~~

Let sleeping dogs…
… lay in your bed - unless they snore! Kate, age 6.

~~~~~~

Bad news travels…
… everywhere! Donovan, age 8.

~~~~~~

Practice what you...
...like to do - like hide from my sister! Jackson, age 5.

~~~~~~

The best things in life are...
... caterpillars.   Christian, age 4.

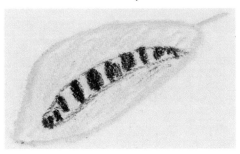

~~~~~~

Silence is...
... only for at church.   Isabella, age 4.

~~~~~~

Once bitten…
… you have to eat the whole thing.   Grayson, age 5.

~~~~~~

You can catch more flies with honey than…
… with a net. Chad, age 4.

~~~~~~

A stitch in time saves…
… your blood. Heather, age 9.

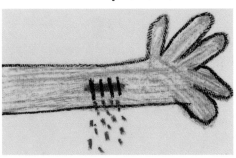

~~~~~~

It's better to be safe than...
... to be dead. Carsen, age 4.

~~~~~~

It's always darkest before...
... you get the flashlight.   Joshua, age 4.

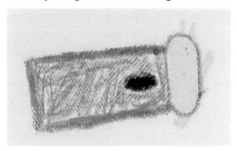

~~~~~~

You can lead a horse to water but...
... you need a string to do it. Thomas, age 4.

~~~~~~

No News is...

... on 32 on the remote.(cartoon channel) Sydney,
age 4.

~~~~~~

A bird in the hand is worth...

... about ten dollars. Cameron, age 4.

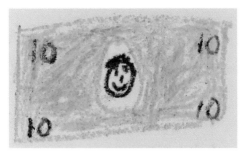

~~~~~~

Two's company, three's...

... this many! (holds up 3 fingers)   Adrian, age 3.

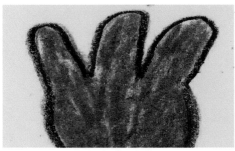

~~~~~~

What's good for the goose, is...
... goose underwear.   Eli, age 5.

~~~~~~

It's never too late to...
... party!   Logan, age 4.

~~~~~~

Give a man enough rope and...
...maybe he will catch a frog. Kaden, age 4.

~~~~~~

The early bird gets...
...the good cereal.   Charles, age 11.

~~~~~~

A miss is as good as a...
... missile.   Hunter, age 3.

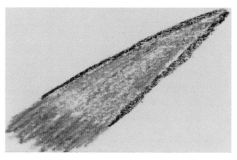

~~~~~~

If you can't beat them...
... just eat the eggs whole. Emma, age 4.

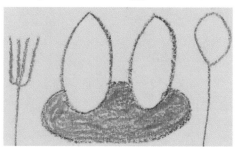

~~~~~~

Let sleeping dogs...
...outside when they wake up.   Landon, age 4.

~~~~~~

Bad news travels...
... all the way to Christmas. Kaitlyn, age 5.

~~~~~~

Practice what you...
...want to ride. Elli, age 5.

~~~~~~

The best things in life are...

... friends. Alec, age 5.

~~~~~~

Silence is...

... good for you. At least that's what my mom says.

Matthew, age 4.

~~~~~~

Once bitten...

... it will leave a spot. Avery, age 4.

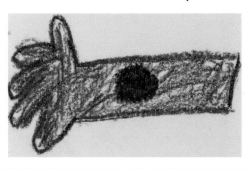

~~~~~~

You can catch more flies with honey than...

... bees.   Claire, age 4.

~~~~~~~~~~~~~~~~~~~~~~~~~~~~~~~~~~~~~~~

Children should be seen & not...

... in the dark without a lantern.   Chase, age 4.

~~~~~~~~~~~~~~~~~~~~~~~~~~~~~~~~~~~~~~~

A stitch in time saves...

... my butt from showing. Drew, age 10.

~~~~~~~~~~~~~~~~~~~~~~~~~~~~~~~~~~~~~~~

ACTUAL PROVERBS (For Reference)

It's better to be safe than sorry.   ~Old English Proverb

Children should be seen & not heard. ~Old English Proverb

It's always darkest before the dawn. ~Old English Proverb

You can lead a horse to water but you cannot make him drink. ~Old English Proverb

No news is good news.   ~French Proverb

A bird in the hand is worth two in the bush. ~Old English Proverb

Two's company, three's a crowd. ~American Proverb

What's good for the goose is good for the gander. ~Originally written as "That that's good sauce for a goose, is good for a gander." in 1670 in John Ray's A Collection of Proverbs.

It's never too late to mend. ~Old English Proverb

Give a man enough rope and he will hang himself. ~Old English Proverb

The early bird gets the worm. ~Old English Proverb

A miss is as good as a mile. ~Old English Proverb

If you can't beat them, join them. ~American idiom based on Scottish proverb

Let sleeping dogs lie. ~Old English Proverb

Bad news travels fast. ~Old English Proverb

The best things in life are free. ~American Proverb

Practice what you preach.   ~Old English Proverb

Silence is golden. ~One half of a German Proverb originally written as - 'Speech is silver, but silence is golden.'

Once bitten, twice shy. ~Old English Proverb

You can catch more flies with honey than vinegar. ~Old English Proverb

A stitch in time saves nine. ~Old English Proverb

BEN FRANKLIN QUOTES

If you lie down with the dogs, you will…
… wake up with dog breath. Anna, age 5.

~~~~~~~~~~~~~~~~~~~~~~~~~~~~~~~~~~~~~~

A fool and his money are…
… my mom & dad at Wesco. Cami, age 4.

~~~~~~~~~~~~~~~~~~~~~~~~~~~~~~~~~~~~~~

People who live in a glass house shouldn't…
… own a bowling ball. Paige, age 8.

~~~~~~~~~~~~~~~~~~~~~~~~~~~~~~~~~~~~~~

A small leak will...
... be a big problem for my dad! Jesse, age 5.

~~~~~~

Early to bed, early to rise, makes a man...
... want to eat French fries?   Laura, age 4.

~~~~~~

A penny saved is...
... kinda like a quarter, only smaller. Josie, age 4.

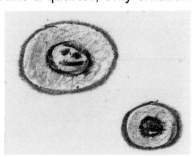

~~~~~~

No pain, no...

... Band-Aids. David, age 4.

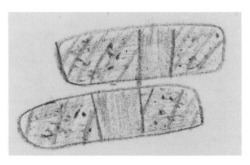

~~~~~~

A fool and his money are...

...like throwing away money in the dumpster.
Noah, age 4.

~~~~~~

If you lie down with the dogs, you will...

... be stinky! Sophia, age 4.

~~~~~~

Three may keep a secret if…
…you glue their mouths shut. Reilly, age 4.

~~~~~~

People who live in a glass house shouldn't…
… walk around in their underwear. Eric, age 6.

~~~~~~

A small leak will…
… get your hat wet. Gus, age 4.

~~~~~~

Early to bed, early to rise, makes a man…

… cry. Benjamin, age 4.

~~~~~~

A penny saved is…

… for a gumball. Morgan, age 3.

~~~~~~

No pain, no…

… super hero stuff. Wesley, age 5.

~~~~~~

After three days, guests, like fish, begin to …

…eat worms? Lily, age 4.

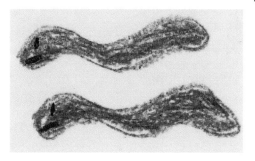

~~~~~~

Never leave until tomorrow what…

… you can throw away today. Whitney, age 5.

~~~~~~

Three may keep a secret if…

…they don't tell me, 'cause I always talk! Riley, age 6.

~~~~~~

ACTUAL BEN FRANKLIN QUOTES
(For Reference)

If you lie down with the dogs, you will rise up with fleas.   ~Benjamin Franklin

A fool and his money are soon parted.
                                        ~Benjamin Franklin

People who live in glass houses shouldn't throw stones.   ~Benjamin Franklin

A small leak can sink a great ship.
                                        ~Benjamin Franklin

Early to bed, early to rise, makes a man healthy, wealthy, and wise.   ~Benjamin Franklin

A penny saved is a penny earned.
                                        ~Benjamin Franklin

No pain, no gain. ~American Adage based on a quote by Benjamin Franklin "There is no gain without pain."

Never leave that till tomorrow that which you can do today.   ~ Benjamin Franklin

Guests, like fish, begin to smell after three days.
                                        ~Benjamin Franklin

Three may keep a secret if two of them are dead.
                                        ~Benjamin Franklin

OTHER FAMOUS SAYINGS AND QUOTES

Where there's smoke, there's...
... my mom cooking hot dogs. Zachary, age 3.

~~~~~~

If at first you don't succeed...
... call the rescue guys. Jake, age 4.

~~~~~~

Don't bite the hand that...
... touches snot. Natalie, age 4.

~~~~~~

The pen is mightier than the...
... strongest crayon. Isabelle, age 5.

~~~~~~

Speak softly and carry a big...
... purse. Shelby, age 4.

~~~~~~

Look before you...
... play in the grass where dogs have been.
Makayla, age 4.

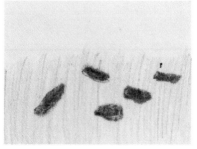

~~~~~~

The only thing we have to fear is…
…mom & dad's eyes when they're mad. Jack, age 4.

~~~~~~

Where there's a will, there's…
… a dead person. Andy, age 12.

~~~~~~

You can't judge a book by…
…ripping it up. You have to read it first. Olivia, age 4.

~~~~~~

You can't teach an old dog…
…to walk on water.   Jakob, age 4.

~~~~~~

If you can't stand the heat…
…put ice in your hat. Michael, age 5.

~~~~~~

The only way to have a friend is to…
…keep your hands to yourself. Brett, age 4.

~~~~~~

Don't cry over...
…thunder, 'cause it's just noise.   Kylie, age 4.

~~~~~~

It ain't over until...
… Christmas. Kyle, age 4.

~~~~~~

The bigger they are, the harder...
… they are to trap. Dallas, age 4.

~~~~~~

It takes two, to…
… play catch. Collyn, age 4.

~~~~~~

When it rains, it…
… waters the flowers. Lindy, age 4.

~~~~~~

Actions speak louder than…
… words on a shirt. Bella, age 4.

~~~~~~

Strike while the…
… cops aren't looking.   Dominique, age 10.

~~~~~~~~~~~~~~~~~~~~~~~~~~~~~~~~~~~~~~~

If at first you don't succeed…
… put batteries in it. Trevor, age 4.

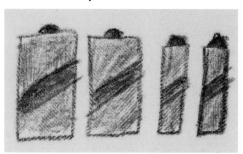

~~~~~~~~~~~~~~~~~~~~~~~~~~~~~~~~~~~~~~~

Eat, drink, and …
… take your vitamins.   Justin, age 7.

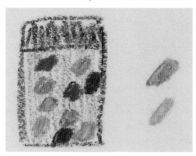

~~~~~~~~~~~~~~~~~~~~~~~~~~~~~~~~~~~~~~~

Never underestimate the power of...
… stinky feet. Christopher, age 4.

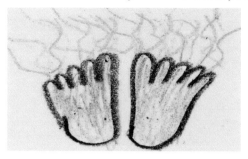

~~~~~~

Where there's smoke, there's...
… a big volcano. Rhiannon, age 4.

~~~~~~

Look before you...
… go to the bathroom in the woods. Joe, age 6.

~~~~~~

Speak softly and carry a big…
… speaker, so they can hear you. Katherine, age 5.

~~~~~~~~~~~~~~~~~~~~~~~~~~~~~~~~~~~~~~~

The pen is mightier than the…
… eraser. Hayden, age 5.

~~~~~~~~~~~~~~~~~~~~~~~~~~~~~~~~~~~~~~~

Don't bite the hand that…
… is Cole's. He will bite you back!   Ryan, age 4.

~~~~~~~~~~~~~~~~~~~~~~~~~~~~~~~~~~~~~~~

The only thing we have to fear is...
... dead bodies. Reider, age 4.

~~~~~~

Where there's a will, there's...
... a boy named William. Tommy, age 5.

~~~~~~

You can't judge a book by...
...the way the teacher reads it. Gracie, age 4.

~~~~~~

You can't teach an old dog...
...not to chew on your pull-ups.   Jimmy, age 4.

~~~~~~

If you can't stand the heat...
...get a fan or something. Colin, age 4.

~~~~~~

The only way to have a friend is to...
...have a lot of money. AJ, age 12.

~~~~~~

Don't cry over...
...what mom says. Just go ask dad. Madison, age 5.

~~~~~~

It ain't over until...
... somebody wins. Erin, age 4.

~~~~~~

The bigger they are, the harder...
... their hair. Brenden, age 4.

~~~~~~

It takes two, to…
… eat a big cake. Dennis, age 7.

~~~~~~

When it rains, it…
… brings a rainbow. Ansley, age 5.

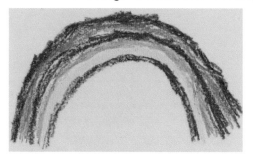

~~~~~~

Actions speak louder than…
… wild cats. Alex, age 4.

~~~~~~

Strike while the...
... ball is close to the bat. Sam, age 4.

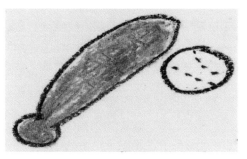

~~~~~~

Eat, drink, and ...
... go poop. Brennan, age 3.

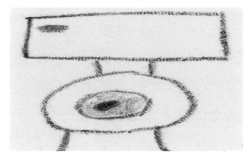

~~~~~~

Never underestimate the power of...
... naked. Kenzie, age 4.

~~~~~~

ACTUAL FAMOUS SAYINGS & QUOTES
(For Reference)

Where there's smoke, there's fire. ~American Adage based on the quote of John Lyly, "There can no great smoke arise, but there must be some fire."

If at first you don't succeed, try, then try again.
~Mason Cooley

Don't bite the hand that feeds you. ~Popular idiom that originated with the Aesop's Fables tale - The Dog in the Manger.

The pen is mightier than the sword.
~Edward Bulwer-Lytton

Speak softly and carry a big stick.
~Theodore Roosevelt

Look before you leap.   ~Samuel Butler
.
The only thing we have to fear is fear itself.
~Franklin D. Roosevelt
Where there's a will, there's a way.
~Général Charles de Gaulle

You can't judge a book by its cover. ~American Idiom based on the writings of François Rabelais, "Don't read only the cheerful titles of books. You have to actually open a book and carefully weigh what's written there."

You can't teach an old dog new tricks.
~E. C. Brewer

If you can't stand the heat get out of the kitchen.
~Harry Truman

The only way to have a friend is to be one.
~Ralph Waldo Emerson

Don't cry over spilt milk.   ~European fairy folklore.
The belief was that fairies enjoyed drinking spilled
milk, so the loss of the spilt milk was for good use and
not a terrible waste.

It ain't over until the fat lady sings. ~Colloquialism
first attributed to sports journalist Ralph Carpenter on
March 10,1976, during the SWC tournament finals.

The bigger they are, the harder they fall.
~American boxer Robert Fitzsimmons in an interview
in 1902.

It takes two to tango.   ~A song title from 1952,
that became a popular American idiom.

When it rains, it pours. ~Sourced from an old
proverb 'It never rains but it pours,' the modern
version, "When it rains, it pours" was the creation of
the Morton Salt company, whose crystallized salt
didn't clump in humid weather.

Actions speak louder than words.
~Abraham Lincoln, 1856

Strike while the iron is hot.   ~Francis Rabelais

Eat, drink and be merry. ~From the Bible,
Ecclesiastes VIII 15 (King James Version)

Never underestimate the power of a woman.
~Popular advertising slogan by *Ladies Home Journal*,
beginning with the March 1941 issue.

###

A NOTE FROM THE AUTHOR

I love hearing from my readers, and I answer all my mail personally. If you enjoyed this book, would you be kind enough to leave a review on Amazon? Even if it's only a few words - it really does make a difference, and would be very much appreciated.

Simply go to www.amazon.com, and type Kristi Porter into the search bar. Then choose the appropriate story, click reviews, create your own review, and let me know what you thought.

~ ~ ~

If you would like to receive an automatic email when my next book is released, go to http://eepurl.com/ES3kD to sign up. Your email address will never be shared and you can unsubscribe at any time.

~ ~ ~

Thanks so much for taking the time to read and review my work. It's readers like you that help make my next book even better!

Kristi Porter

OTHER BOOKS BY KRISTI PORTER

Available at Amazon.com and bookstores everywhere.

How to Tell When You're Really Old - Funny Happens When Kids Define Old Age, is the result of hundreds of interviews with children ages three to twelve, who were asked to explain how they could tell when someone was really old. Their candid, uncensored, and often hilarious answers will not only make you rethink the aging process, but are sure to become instant favorites for readers of all ages.

~ ~ ~

Babies Come From… Where?!? Funny Happens When Kids Explain Pregnancy & Birth is the result of hundreds of interviews with children ages three to twelve, who were simply asked "Where do you think babies come from?" and allowed to answer freely, giving as much or as little explanation as they saw fit. Now, their candid, uncensored and often hilarious answers have been collected and made available for all to enjoy in this delightful little book that is sure to be a favorite for years to come.

~ ~ ~

Priceless Proverbs - Book 2, is the second volume of the wildly popular Priceless Proverbs Collection. It features over one hundred additional quotes - wise, entertaining and uncensored - by kids ages three to twelve who were asked to finish well-known proverbs or famous sayings all on their own. Great for anyone that loves children or simply needs a smile to brighten their day.

~ ~ ~

Stranger Danger - How to Talk to Kids About Strangers is a guide to help parents and caregivers of children ages 3-8 teach kids about strangers in a fun, interactive, and age appropriate way - without scaring them. This easy to read, step by step guide gives parents age appropriate words and activities to use with even the youngest of children. Covering everything from who is a stranger, to when and how to fight back, *Stranger Danger - How to Talk to Kids About Strangers* is a must read guide for today's parents.

~ ~ ~

ABOUT THE AUTHOR

Kristi Porter has over twenty-five years of experience working with young children, both as a preschool teacher, and as an award winning child care provider. She holds a degree in Early Childhood Education and Development, as well as a national Child Development Associate Credential. In 1999, she was awarded the Governor's Quality Care Award for her outstanding commitment to the care and education of young children.

Always a reader, Kristi never thought much about writing until she entered a writing contest sponsored by the Detroit Free Press. Her story - *The Worst Vacation Ever* - went on to be published in a travel anthology that was distributed worldwide. This was followed by numerous articles published in local magazines and newspapers. As her love of writing grew, she added adult fiction, how-to books for parents, and short humor pieces to her repertoire.

But kids and writing aren't all Kristi relishes. She also enjoys bicycling, video games, photography, Facebook, and spending time with family. She lives in Michigan.

CONNECT WITH KRISTI ONLINE

Twitter: @KristiPorter3

Facebook: Facebook/Kristi Porter - Author

Website: http://happikamper.weebly.com

Email: Kristiporter03@gmail.com

ACKNOWLEDGEMENTS

I'd like to extend a warm thanks to Lynn Dahl Scholl, Tish Huber Winton, and Sheri Berge, for helping me conduct hundreds of interviews with children over the years. I couldn't have done it without all of you.

Many thanks as well to the White Lake Writers Group for their guidance, encouragement, and support as I sorted through all of those interviews to put this book together.

A special thanks goes out to Tirzah Goodwin, for her awesome cover design; & to my three amazing grandsons for their help with illustrations.

Lots of love, respect and appreciation to my husband for his understanding and support as I spent countless hours in front of the computer, preparing this book for publication.

And to my mom, for always believing in me, encouraging me, and pestering me to finish this and other projects - I love you more than words can say.

And finally, a heartfelt thank you to the children of North Muskegon, who allowed me into their hearts and minds, and gave me a remarkable glimpse into this wonderful world we live in - thru their eyes, their minds, and their perceptions. Priceless.

Printed in Great Britain
by Amazon.co.uk, Ltd.,
Marston Gate.